j796.332 Kennedy, Mike (Mike
KEN   William)

        Football.

$25.50   Grades 2-3   10/31/2006

DATE			

Football

Football

Mike Kennedy

$\mathcal{W\!atts}$ LIBRARY™

Franklin Watts
A Division of Scholastic Inc.
New York • Toronto • London • Auckland • Sydney
Mexico City • New Delhi • Hong Kong
Danbury, Connecticut

Note to readers: Definitions for words in **bold** can be found in the Glossary at the back of this book.

Photographs © 2003: AP/Wide World Photos: 42 (Jean-Marc Bouju), 28 (Michael Conroy), 18 (John Gaps III), 43 (Tony Gutierrez), 5 left, 26 (Ann Heisenfelt), 25 (Linda Kaye), 50 (Mark Lennihan), 15 (Milwaukee Journal Sentinel), 36 (Gene J. Puskar), 34 (Mike Roemer), 24 (John Russell), 38 (Reed Saxon), 6 (Gregory Smith), 49 (John Swart), 30 (Winslow Townson), 5 right, 20 (David Zalubowski), 14, 16, 44; Corbis Images: 8, 12, 13, 47 (Bettmann), cover (Duomo), 2 (Reuters NewMedia Inc.), 40, 41 (Oscar White); Getty Images: 33 (Elsa), 51 (Donald Miralle); Icon Sports Media: 27 (Tom Hauck), 29 (Wireimage.com), 48; Pop Warner: 10.

The photograph opposite the title page shows Deion Sanders (#21) intercepting a pass during an NFL game.

Library of Congress Cataloging-in-Publication Data

Kennedy, Mike (Mike William), 1965–
    Football / by Mike Kennedy.
      p. cm. — (Watts library)
    Summary: Discusses the sport of football including its history, rules and regulations, game bowls, and some outstanding players.
    Includes bibliographical references and index.
    ISBN 0-531-12272-7 (lib. bdg.)   0-531-15589-7 (pbk.)
    1. Football—Juvenile literature. [1. Football.] I. Title. II. Series.
GV950.7.K46 2003
796.332—dc21

2003000123

Contents

While it remains a physical sport, football is not nearly as violent as it was in its early days.

Chapter One

A Hard-Hitting Story

Football as you know it has been more than 150 years in the making. Students at Harvard University got the ball rolling in the first half of the nineteenth century. They enjoyed the British sport of rugby and played an annual match called "Bloody Monday." These rough and dangerous contests helped lay the groundwork for football. But it wasn't until after the Civil War that the modern version of the sport started to take shape.

Drawing a Line

The generation of American men who came of age in the 1870s grew up on tales of **valor** from the battlefield. In school they studied science and learned that a healthy body was essential for a healthy mind. They also discovered the joys of team sports. Baseball was their favorite, and they played every spring and summer. But when the weather turned cool each autumn, they searched for other sports to amuse them.

Football appealed to college students because it featured all the **tactics** and romance of war. Back then the sport had few rules and was very disorganized. In 1874, a team from McGill University in Canada taught players from Harvard a more sophisticated version that used an egg-shaped ball. Two years later, Harvard, Princeton, Yale, and Columbia formed the

Students from Yale's football team gather for a photo in the late 19th century.

Intercollegiate Football Association (IFA) with the hope of bringing order to the sport.

No one believed in the IFA's goals more than a Yale University student named Walter Camp. In fact he dedicated his life to football. In 1880, Camp proposed a new rule that established the line of scrimmage. This imaginary barrier—which separates the offense and defense—distinguished football from all similar team sports, especially rugby. Camp also pushed through rules that gave the offense a series of downs to move the ball, and limited each side to eleven players.

Camp's **ingenuity** helped make football a popular spectator sport. Colleges nationwide started teams, and coaches and players began devising set plays on offense and defense. Since the forward pass was not yet part of the game, running with the ball and kicking it were football's most important skills. But a rule passed in 1888 that allowed tackling below the waist threatened to halt the sport's progress in its tracks. Advancing the ball was already so difficult that runners often pulled up in the backfield and punted on first or second down. Now defenses dominated completely, and football **degenerated** into a plodding test of brute strength.

What's the Score?

The scoring system used in football has changed a great deal over the years. Originally, a safety counted for one point, a touchdown for two, a successful kick after a touchdown for four, and a goal kicked from the field (field goal) for five.

Pop Culture

Glenn "Pop" Warner was one of football's true pioneers. He starred for Cornell University in the 1890s and later coached the University of Pittsburgh to two national championships. In between, he also coached the famous Carlisle Indian Industrial School. His innovations included the single- and double-wing formations, screen pass, three-point stance, jerseys with numbers, and the use of shoulder and thigh pads. In 1929, he founded Pop Warner Football, which today is the nation's largest youth league.

Safety First

Before long, critics complained that football was too dangerous. Players didn't use helmets and wore little padding to protect their bodies. Coaches were experimenting with bone-crunching offensive formations such as the Flying

Wedge. In these types of mass plays, a ball carrier moved downfield surrounded by a human chain of blockers. Serious injuries occurred regularly on the gridiron, and deaths were reported every year.

In 1904, President Theodore Roosevelt threatened to ban football if drastic safety reforms weren't instituted. Colleges formed the Intercollegiate Athletic Association (IAA)—the forerunner to the National Collegiate Athletic Association (NCAA)—to create a safer game. Among the rules they approved was the legalization of the forward pass. This forced players to spread out more on the field and made most mass plays obsolete.

Going Pro

Under the IAA's guidance, college football became a major sport. The professional game, meanwhile, was successful only in small pockets of Pennsylvania and Ohio. Though collegiate stars (playing under fake names) had begun accepting money from semi-pro teams as early as 1893, a serious attempt to start a national pro league wasn't made until 1920. It was called the American Professional Football Association, but changed its name to the National Football League (NFL) in time for the 1922 season.

The NFL struggled for many years to lure fans to its Sunday games. Many collegiate stars chose to coach at universities rather than enter the play-for-pay world. When All-Americans such as Red Grange, Bronko Nagurski, Benny

Your Move

Ironically, the Flying Wedge was conceived in 1892 by a chess expert and military historian named Lorin Deland.

Red Grange (far left) looks for an opening in the defense. In the 1920s, the "Galloping Ghost" drew thousands of fans to the NFL with his exciting running style.

Friedman, Wildcat Wilson, and Ernie Nevers signed contracts, the pro game received a tremendous boost. Grange, nicknamed the Galloping Ghost, made the biggest headlines when he accompanied the Chicago Bears on a nationwide tour in 1925 and 1926. The Bears sold out every stadium they visited, Grange thrilled fans with his electrifying play, and pro football started to gain respect.

College football, however, remained the fan favorite. In the 1920s, as America's obsession with sports grew, attendance at college games rose, and gridiron stars attained almost **mythical** status. No school had a larger following than Notre Dame. Coached by Knute Rockne—a master motivator, strategist, and promoter—the Fighting Irish played anyone, anywhere, and won just about every time they took the field. Fans mourned in 1931 when Rockne died in a plane crash. His career record at the time was 105–12–5, including five unbeaten and untied seasons.

Notre Dame became a national powerhouse under Knute Rockne (seated, right), the most innovative coach of his era.

Passing Fancy

The Great Depression of the 1930s hit America hard, but college football continued to thrive. Games were broadcast on radio, the Associated Press began providing weekly rankings of the nation's best teams, and magazines published preseason guides touting top players. By the 1940s, the tradition of New Year's Day bowl games had taken root, and awards such as the Heisman Trophy had grown in prestige.

Welcome Back

From 1934 through 1945 not a single African-American played professional football. In 1946, Kenny Washington broke this color barrier playing for the Los Angeles Rams. By the 1950s, African-Americans such as Marion Motley, Dick Lane, Emlen Tunnell, John Henry Johnson, Horace Gillom, Bill Willis, Tank Younger, and Buddy Young were considered among the NFL's best and toughest players.

During the same period, the NFL tried to keep pace by adopting rules to increase scoring. The league switched to a smaller ball that was easier to throw and catch. The changes worked, as quarterback Sammy Baugh and receiver Don Hutson ushered in an exciting **aerial** style of play.

In 1946, the All-American Football Conference (AAFC) appeared on the scene. The league established franchises in cities new to professional sports such as Los Angeles, San

Francisco, and Miami. In response, the NFL expanded, and eventually absorbed the AAFC. This set the stage for a fresh generation of stars, including quarterbacks Otto Graham and Norm Van Brocklin and runners Hugh McElhenney and Frank Gifford.

Super Men

Joe Namath energized professional football when he made good on his bold prediction to win the Super Bowl in 1969.

Professional football received a major boost in 1958 when millions of television viewers watched the Baltimore Colts win the NFL championship in a thrilling overtime game. Two years later, the league hired Pete Rozelle as commissioner. The 33-year-old marketing whiz cashed in on the NFL's growing popularity by **negotiating** a national television con-

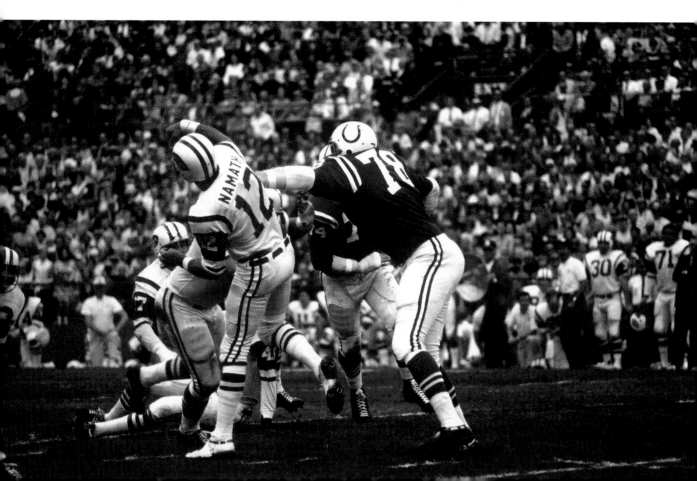

Vince and the Pack

No team embodied the **topsy-turvy** 1960s better than the Green Bay Packers. Coach Vince Lombardi was the ultimate disciplinarian and a throwback to more conservative times. His players were free spirits embracing new lifestyles and attitudes. Somehow the Packers meshed perfectly. From 1961 to 1967, Green Bay was crowned NFL champion five times.

tract with CBS. The deal earned millions for the owners, and turned players such as Jim Brown, Johnny Unitas, and Paul Hornung into household names.

Meanwhile, the NFL faced a new challenge from the American Football League (AFL). The league began play in 1960, and its rich owners often outbid the NFL for college stars such as Billy Cannon, Buck Buchanan, and Joe Namath. In 1966, Rozelle ended the mounting hostilities and announced plans for a merger. Part of the deal called for the leagues to play for the championship of pro football each year. The Green Bay Packers demonstrated the NFL's superiority by dominating the first two title contests. But when Namath led the New York Jets to a shocking upset of the Baltimore Colts in Super Bowl III, the AFL showed its **mettle**, and pro football entered a new era of prosperity.

The NFL completely absorbed the AFL by 1970, and the league was divided into two conferences, the National Football Conference and American Football Conference. Nine years later, the NFL expanded to twenty-eight teams. Meanwhile, charismatic stars such as Walter Payton, Joe Montana,

Perfect!

The 1972 Miami Dolphins was the only team in NFL history to go undefeated. They went 17–0, including a 14–7 victory over the Washington Redskins in Super Bowl VII.

Few quarterbacks in NFL history have matched Joe Montana's poise or flair for the dramatic.

and Lawrence Taylor drew new fans to the sport. And the rise of dynasties by the Pittsburgh Steelers, Dallas Cowboys, and San Francisco 49ers helped turn the Super Bowl into the nation's most watched sporting event.

As the NFL's popularity exploded, college coaches saw their world changing before their eyes. The process had started in the 1960s, when schools that had traditionally ignored black athletes opened their doors to African-Americans. Eventually, amateur stars began to view college as a stepping-stone to the pros.

Collegiate players today are bigger, stronger, and faster than ever. Many choose to leave school early for the riches of the NFL. Three college programs—the University of Miami, University of Florida, and Florida State University—regularly produce the best pro prospects. In turn they attract the nation's most talented high school players, and annually finish at or near the top of the national rankings.

Despite these dramatic changes, football's appeal continues to grow. The Super Bowl draws more than 100 million television viewers worldwide. The top college programs generate

High School Heroes

High school football has a long and glorious tradition. Some programs took root as far back as the 1870s, and more players have competed in high school than in college and the pros combined. Many schools field three different teams: freshman, junior varsity, and varsity. According to estimates, more than one million boys and girls play high school football today. For many, this is the last chance to compete on the gridiron. A small percentage of players moves on to a college program, and far fewer make it to the NFL.

millions of dollars for their schools. (Revenues run so high that some people argue collegiate players should be paid.) Youth football leagues attract hundreds of thousands of boys and girls every year. Video games like "Madden NFL" and "NCAA Football" have been among the hottest sellers on the market.

This really shouldn't surprise anyone. Football was born in the minds of young people inspired by tales of heroism and valor, and this spirit lives on in players and fans today. In fact, some say football's future is brighter than ever.

A running back breaks into the clear during a college football game.

Chapter Two

Role Call

A player who's big and strong, but not very fast or **coordinated**, probably wouldn't make a good wide receiver. But put him on the defensive line and he can be a star. History also shows that a place-kicker can be just as valuable to his team as the starting quarterback. That's one of the great things about football. The roles on every team are as varied as the athletes needed to fill them.

Take Your Position

Eleven players from each team line up on every play. The team on offense tries to

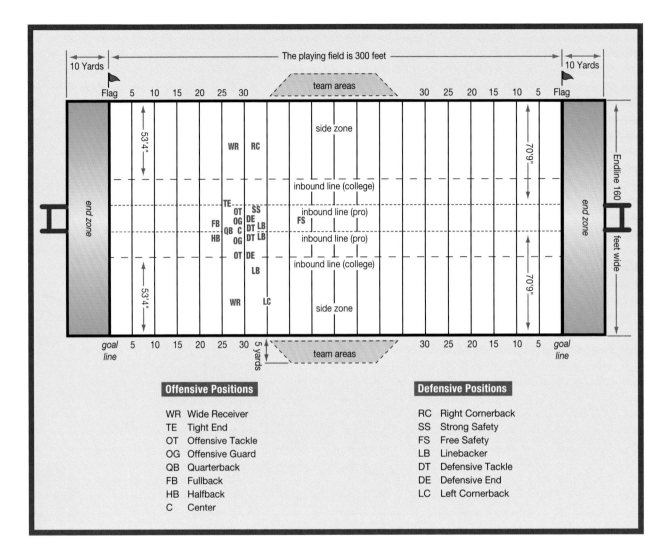

The playing field is 300 feet

10 Yards   10 Yards

Flag   5   10   15   20   25   30   team areas   30   25   20   15   10   5   Flag

side zone

53'4"   WR   RC   70'9"

inbound line (college)

TE   SS   inbound line (pro)
OT DE
OG DT LB
FB QB C   FS
HB   OG DT LB   inbound line (pro)
OT DE   inbound line (college)

LB

WR   LC   side zone

goal   5   10   15   20   25   30   5 yards   team areas   30   25   20   15   10   5   goal
line   line

end zone   end zone

Endline 160 feet wide

Offensive Positions

WR	Wide Receiver
TE	Tight End
OT	Offensive Tackle
OG	Offensive Guard
QB	Quarterback
FB	Fullback
HB	Halfback
C	Center

Defensive Positions

RC	Right Cornerback
SS	Strong Safety
FS	Free Safety
LB	Linebacker
DT	Defensive Tackle
DE	Defensive End
LC	Left Cornerback

move the ball downfield into scoring position. The team on defense tries to stop them.

What are the most common formations? On offense, it's the quarterback, two running backs (halfback and fullback), two wide receivers (split end and flanker), tight end, and five linemen (two tackles, two guards, and a center). On defense, it's four linemen (two tackles and two ends), three linebackers (one middle and two outside), and four defensive backs (two cornerbacks and two safeties).

There are variations within these sets. For example, some defensive coaches prefer to play three linemen and four linebackers. Some offenses, meanwhile, use three running backs and just one receiver.

Coaches are allowed to make substitutions between plays. On third and long, the offense might send in extra receivers for the halfback and fullback. Expecting such a move, the defense might replace one or two linebackers with additional defensive backs.

Whether a starter or reserve, a player never takes the field without the proper equipment. Football pants include special pockets for knee and thigh pads, while other padding fits

Players in youth leagues and high school are required to wear full protective gear.

comfortably against the hips. Rib and shoulder pads protect the areas suggested by their names. The helmet and mouth guard prevent head injuries.

Skilled Labor

Players who handle the ball are said to play skill positions. They rely a great deal on speed, quickness, good hands, and shifty moves. Quarterback, running back, receiver, and defensive back all fall into this category.

There's a misconception that all a quarterback needs is a strong arm. Don't believe it. A sharp mind and good leadership skills are far more important. The quarterback runs the offense. He calls the plays in the huddle, and shouts out **audibles** at the line of scrimmage. Teams respond best to a signal caller who has earned their total confidence.

Running backs line up in the backfield behind the quarterback. Good runners are **elusive** and hard to tackle. They sense openings in the defense and burst through them without hesitation. They also rarely fumble. What's the proper technique for carrying the ball? Tuck it snugly between your forearm and

body. Keep your hand on one of the points of the ball and your elbow over the other.

When the quarterback drops back to pass, he scans the field for a wide receiver, tight end, or running back breaking

As this picture demonstrates, the quarterback (kneeling) commands the full attention of everyone on offense.

Get a Grip

To throw a pass with a tight spiral, grip the ball near one of the ends where it narrows. Place your pinky, ring finger, and middle finger on the laces, and cup the point of the ball between your thumb and index finger. When releasing the ball, let it spin out of your hand, and complete the throwing motion by following through with your arm across your body.

A running back cradles the ball in his left arm as he avoids a tackle at the line of scrimmage.

into the clear. What's the key to getting open? Speed helps, but running precise and deceptive pass routes is essential. Make a defender believe you're going to sprint in one direction, then break back to the exact spot where the quarterback expects you to be.

Catching the ball takes concentration and sure hands. Watch the pass the moment the quarterback releases it. Snatch the ball with your hands rather than trapping it against your pads. After the catch, cradle the ball against your body.

Defensive backs try to shut down the passing game. In zone coverage, they are assigned areas of the field and told to guard anyone who enters their space. In one-on-one coverage, each defensive back shadows a specific receiver. Playing in the defensive backfield (or "secondary") is difficult if you can't run backward smoothly, and stop and start quickly.

In the Trenches

When announcers refer to the battle in the trenches, they're talking about the clashes along the line of scrimmage. Being a lineman or playing linebacker calls for a combination of raw power and sound technique. The offensive line tries to open holes on running plays and protect the quarterback on passes.

The backers and defensive line try to clog up the line of scrimmage and penetrate into the backfield. (Linebackers also drop back in pass coverage.) Don't underestimate these players. Their performance often determines which team wins.

What's the number one rule when blocking and tackling? Keep your head up and your eyes on your target. Hitting an opponent with the top of your helmet is extremely dangerous.

Blocking is a matter of leverage. The key to driving an opponent backward is getting lower than he is and maintaining that advantage. How is this done? Look straight ahead and stay balanced by bending your knees slightly and keeping your feet shoulder-width apart. When firing into a defender, use your arms to thrust your upper body and shoulders forward. After initial contact, take short, choppy steps to push your opponent back.

The battles between offensive and defensive linemen are always hard-nosed.

Tackling isn't much different—except that defenders can wrap their arms around the ball carrier and use their hands to pull him down. In fact, when all else fails, grab hold of the ball carrier's jersey, and don't let go. This will give teammates time to hustle over and help out.

In the NFL, it usually takes more than one defender to bring down a ball carrier.

Something Special

The players who enter the game in punting and kicking situations are known collectively as the special teams. These squads are often made up of less experienced players hoping to impress the coaches. But this doesn't mean that special teams are unimportant. On the contrary, punting and kicking mistakes can spell the difference between winning and losing.

During a kickoff or punt, the team booting the ball away sprints downfield at full speed in pursuit of the returner. The team returning the kick tries to advance the ball as far as possible. (Of course, on some punts and almost every field goal attempt, the defense's goal is to block the kick.)

Returning kickoffs and punts takes skill and guts. The first challenge is catching the ball. Then the trick is to get up field as quickly as possible. Returners who make too many fakes usually don't get very far.

The punter and place-kicker are the most **prominent** members of the special teams. Just because both players only have to kick the ball, don't think for a second that their jobs are easy. The pressure on punters and place-kickers is immense. That's why they spend so much time practicing their form.

Lots of fans watch the ball on kickoffs and punts—as well as during all other plays. But here's a good tip: Keep one eye on the field. Teams execute set plays on every down. Following where the players move will help you understand the game. And that's one of keys to learning how to play better.

The place-kicker faces tremendous pressure every time he attempts a field goal.

The excitement is usually non-stop when the action starts in an NFL game.

Chapter Three

Game Time

The object in football is to score more points than the opponent. Games are divided into four quarters, each one running fifteen minutes in college and the NFL. (Games are shorter in high school and youth leagues.) Teams change directions at the end of each quarter. The first two quarters make up the first half, and the second two make up the second half. Teams are given a rest period midway through the game called halftime. Some leagues, including the NFL, play **overtime** if a game is tied at the end of the fourth quarter.

Getting Started

A football field is rectangular, with two end zones measuring 10 yards (9 meters) long. Goal lines extend across the front of each end zone. The white lines stretching the length of the field are sidelines. Those at the back of the end zone are endlines. A ball carrier is out of bounds as soon as he touches or goes beyond a sideline or endline.

Each team is challenged to protect its end zone. Carrying the ball across the enemy's goal line or catching a pass in the end zone is a touchdown (6 points). Kicking the ball between the enemy's goal posts—which are located at the back of each end zone—and above the crossbar is a field goal (three points). Tackling a ball carrier in his own end zone is a safety (two points). Safeties are also recorded when a player fumbles the ball out of his end zone or when a blocked punt bounces out of the end zone.

After a touchdown, the ball is placed at the 3-yard (2.7 m) line, and the offense is given a choice. The safest option is booting the ball through the goal posts for the extra point. The offense can also go for the riskier two-point conversion, getting only one play to move the ball across the goal line.

Toss Up

Every football game begins with a coin toss to determine which team will kickoff. The team that receives the kick gets set to go on offense. The other prepares to play defense.

The team on offense gets four downs to advance the ball at

Counting Down

Starting at midfield, each side of the field counts yardage backward to the goal line. That's why every NFL field has two 40-, 30-, 20-, and 10-yard (37-, 27-, 18-, and 9-meter) lines.

least 10 yards (9 m). Every time the offense makes the necessary yardage, it is awarded a new series of downs. If the offense fails to move 10 yards (9 m) in four plays, the opposition gains possession of the football. That's why teams usually punt on fourth down. It's much smarter to boot the ball downfield and force the opponent deeper in its territory.

On every play, the offense must have seven players on the line of scrimmage. All seven must stay perfectly still until the

Wildlife

Referees are nicknamed zebras because they wear black-and-white striped shirts. But don't let this nickname fool you. Referees are crucial in organized football. They are responsible for enforcing the rules. When they spot an **infraction**, they toss a yellow flag in the direction of the guilty party. This indicates that someone has done something illegal and his team is about to be penalized.

Defenders are not allowed to grab a ball carrier's face mask when attempting to make a tackle.

ball is snapped. Players positioned behind the line are permitted to move, but only one at a time and they can't go forward.

Blocking penalties are the costliest for the offense. Grabbing a defender and pulling him to the ground is holding. Hitting a defender in the back is clipping. Knocking a defender off balance with a kick to his legs is tripping. All these penalties cancel out any yardage gained, and move the offense back at least 10 yards (9 m).

Penalties can be equally damaging to the defense. Jumping across the line of scrimmage and making contact with a player on offense is offsides. Holding is called when a defender clutches a receiver as he sprints downfield. Bumping a receiver while a pass is in the air is interference. Tackling penalties include facemasking (grabbing a player's face mask) and spearing (using the top of your helmet to hit a player). Knocking down the quarterback after he has thrown the ball is roughing the passer. (It is also illegal to run into a kicker or punter after he has booted the ball.) All these penalties give the offense extra yardage, and can result in an automatic first down.

Teams don't have to accept penalties. The action continues when a flag is thrown after the ball is snapped. For example, if a defender is flagged for facemasking near the goal line but the ball carrier lunges into the end zone, the offense will decline the penalty and take the six points.

Ball Control

What's more troublesome for the offense than penalties? Fumbles and interceptions. A fumble occurs when a runner drops the ball before a referee whistles that the play has ended. Hard tackles force most fumbles, but sometimes a player simply loses control of the football.

A fumble is a free ball. Anyone can recover it. Defenders often try to scoop up a fumble and take off for the end zone. Players on offense are usually happy to fall on the ball and

When a player fumbles the ball, anyone on the offense or defense can recover it.

keep possession. If a fumble goes out of bounds, the team that last controlled it gets to keep it.

An interception occurs when a defender catches a forward pass. In the NFL, a reception is legal only if the receiver controls the ball with both feet in bounds. Only one foot inbounds is needed in college, high school, and youth leagues. A pass is ruled incomplete if it skips off the turf or if the receiver drops the ball before establishing control of it.

Fumbles recovered by the opposition and interceptions are known as turnovers. They often change the course of a game. In fact, more times than not, the team with fewer turnovers comes out on top. Of course, the same is true of the team that commits the fewest penalties.

Forward and Backward

A **forward pass** must be attempted from behind the line of scrimmage. If not, it is a penalty. On the other hand, a backward pass or **lateral** can be attempted anywhere on the field. But like a fumble, it is a free ball.

GRAND MARSHAL

The Tournament of Roses parade, held every year before the Rose Bowl, is one of college sports' greatest traditions.

Symbols of America

Chapter Four

Bowled Over

The Super Bowl decides the NFL champion. It is the biggest football game of the year, but not the only bowl game. There are more than two dozen college bowls contested every December and January.

Coming up Roses

How did football get so "bowl crazy"? The tradition began in Pasadena, California, as part of a New Year's festival known as the Tournament of Roses, which offered a **smorgasbord** of sporting events. Officials decided to try football, and on January 1, 1902, Michigan traveled west and routed Stanford 49–0.

Though the game was a hit with fans, the Tournament of Roses dropped football in favor of other sports, including polo and chariot races. In 1916, the game was **reinstated**, and soon became the nation's most anticipated college sporting event. It wasn't until 1928, however, that the annual contest was dubbed the "Rose Bowl."

The name took "rose" from Tournament of Roses and "bowl" from the look of the new stadium in Pasadena where the game had been moved in 1923. The arena featured a large grass field surrounded by high-reaching stands. Connecticut's Yale Bowl, which had the appearance of a huge bowl, was its inspiration.

The Yale Bowl, shown here in 1915, was one of college football's first modern stadiums.

Soon other New Year's Day bowl games were introduced. All were named for a state **symbol**: the Orange Bowl in Florida and the Sugar Bowl in Louisiana (both 1935); the Cotton Bowl in Texas (1937); the Gator Bowl, also in Florida (1946).

Originally, college bowls were like big parties for the nation's best teams. The games made lots of money for the cities hosting them and offered a great way for people to show **civic** pride. But a new emphasis was placed on bowl games in the 1940s after the media began naming a college football national champion. Once bowl organizers realized that their game might decide the title, they scrambled to sign deals with the country's most powerful conferences.

College football fans are sometimes more intense than the players they're cheering for.

Who's #1?

Over the years, determining the nation's top college team got more and more difficult. Voters didn't always agree, and there were no set criteria to guide them. Sometimes one media poll named a team number one, while another poll recognized a different school. This made the bowl picture very confusing.

Look at Me

Several "all-star" bowl games are held every year, including the Senior Bowl, Hula Bowl, East-West Shrine Game, and Blue-Gray Game. These contests are excellent opportunities for NFL coaches and scouts to evaluate players headed for the pros.

The NCAA took steps to clarify things in 1998 by adopting the Bowl Championship Series (BCS). This system uses a computer to rank the best teams. At season's end, the top two meet in the Rose Bowl, Sugar Bowl, Orange Bowl, or Fiesta Bowl. The winner takes the national title. All the other bowl games are still held, but teams play mostly for school pride.

Is the BCS perfect? No. Some critics want college football to use a playoff system. Others want to go back to the old voting method. For them, arguing about "who's number one" is a tradition unto itself.

Super Sunday

There's never any debate when it comes to crowning pro football's champion. The Super Bowl, first held in 1967, is the finale of the NFL's postseason tournament. The playoffs start with twelve teams, six from the NFC and six from the AFC. They battle down to two finalists, and the conference champs meet for the title.

The Super Bowl is held in a different location every year. The excitement surrounding the game is unparalleled. Television and newspaper reporters from all over the world cover the contest. Hundreds of millions of fans tune into the game on television. The pressure is incredible. Great plays are remembered forever. Bonehead mistakes are never forgotten. For professionals, there is no bigger thrill than playing in the Super Bowl—and no sweeter feeling than winning one.

The Vince Lombardi trophy, professional football's most prized possession, is presented annually to the NFL team that wins the Super Bowl.

Aloha!

The NFL Pro Bowl—held in Hawaii at the end of each season—pits the best players from the NFC and against the best from the AFC.

*Jim Thorpe, a
Native American,
was one of football's
first superstars.*

Chapter Five

Movers and Shakers

Thousands of players have competed in the NFL. Many thousands more have played in college. What separates the unforgettable ones? Statistics are one way to compare stars of different generations. But there's an even better measuring stick: Did a player change the way football was played? Here's a look at those who have done just that.

From Pudge to the Ghost

William "Pudge" Heffelfinger starred on Yale's offensive line from 1888 to 1891, earning All-American honors three times. At 6 feet 3 (191 centimeters) and 205 pounds (92 kilograms), Pudge was a giant in his day and used his size to full advantage. Amazingly quick, he was the first guard to race from his position on the line and clear a path around the end for a running back.

One runner who didn't need a blocker was Jim Thorpe. From 1911 to 1920, he was the best ball carrier (and probably the greatest athlete) in North America. He also punted and played defense better than anyone. Thorpe perfected the technique of catching kicks while sprinting at full speed, making it nearly impossible for oncoming tacklers to stop him.

Red Grange ran with a similar combination of power and imagination. The "Galloping Ghost" was a spectacular college

Pioneering Pro

In 1915, Frederick "Fritz" Pollard led Brown University to the Rose Bowl and was named All-American at running back. His accomplishments were all the more notable because he was African-American. In Pollard's day, earning the respect of his white peers was extremely difficult.

After serving in World War I, he joined the Akron Pros of the Ohio League. Pollard established himself as one of professional football's premier running backs—despite the attempts of opponents to injure him. To **discourage** players from piling on top of him after a tackle, he would roll on to his back and stick his cleats straight in the air. Pollard's ingenuity and **tenacity** obviously impressed management. In 1921 Akron made him the first black head coach in pro football history.

player, but it was his impact on pro football that was most dramatic. In fact, the struggling NFL might have collapsed had he not signed with the Chicago Bears in 1925.

From Cal to Brown

Cal Hubbard set the stage for today's hulking offensive tackles. At 6 feet 6 (198 cm), he stood a foot taller than most men of his generation and was also fast and agile. From 1927 to 1936, Hubbard played on four NFL championship teams.

"Slingin'" Sammy Baugh was football's first modern passer. Though he cradled the ball in an unusual way and often threw sidearm, the "Texas Tornado" could fire short tosses and long bombs with equal accuracy. During his career with the Washington Redskins (1937 to 1952), quarterback became the most important position in football.

Cal Hubbard was big, fast and strong— and the best offensive lineman of his era.

Over the same period, wide receivers developed into offensive threats, thanks to players like Don Hutson. Before he joined the Green Bay Packers in 1935, ends spent most of their time blocking downfield on running plays. By his retirement in 1945, they were the primary targets in the passing game. Hutson posted 99 touchdown receptions during his career, a mark that stood for more than fifty years.

Dick "Night Train" Lane was one of few players who could have covered Hutson. Bigger and stronger than most receivers he faced, Lane introduced a new way to play cornerback, utilizing his muscle to knock pass-catchers off their patterns. His 14 interceptions during his 1952 rookie year are still a record.

Jim Brown was the most feared runner ever to take the field—and caused coaches to rethink defensive strategy. From 1957 to 1965 with the Cleveland Browns, he rushed for 12,312 yards (11,080 m). No single tackler could bring him down. This forced teams to commit more players to the line of scrimmage, which created better passing opportunities for the Cleveland offense.

From Johnny U. to Sweetness

Johnny Unitas proved no lead was safe. Regardless of how little time remained on the clock, the tough and talented quarterback could guide his team into scoring position. "Johnny U." holds the record for consecutive games (47) with a touchdown pass. One of his favorite targets on the Baltimore Colts in the 1960s was John Mackey. Quick and sure-handed, Mackey demonstrated the value of a tight end as a receiver. This tandem inspired people to look at the passing game in a new way.

When Johnny Unitas stood under center, opposing defenses always had to be on their toes.

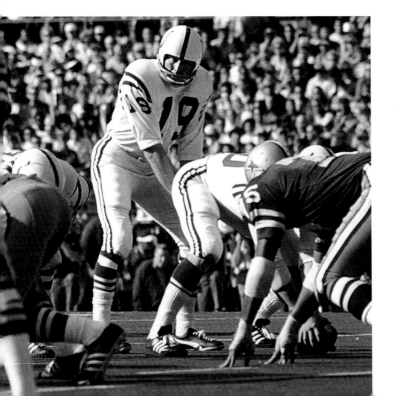

48

Walter Payton, nicknamed "Sweetness," was a pure joy to watch when he had the ball.

David "Deacon" Jones was a quarterback's worst nightmare. A member of the 1960s defensive front known as the Fearsome Foursome, he never gave up on a play. His relentless pursuit of opposing quarterbacks glamorized the **sack**, which years later became an official statistic. Dick Butkus, the middle linebacker for the Chicago Bears from 1965 to 1973, intimidated opponents just by stepping on the field. The NFL has never seen a meaner or more ferocious player.

Walter Payton was a hard-nosed back in the 1970s and 1980s who combined old-time, smash-mouth football with the speed of today's game. "Sweetness" never shied away from contact, but was also a beautiful runner in the open field. His career record of 16,726 rushing yards (15, 053 m) stood until Emmitt Smith of the Dallas Cowboys broke it in October 2002.

Heck of a Guy

Ray Guy of the Oakland Raiders showed how much a punter could influence the outcome of a game. His high, angled punts consistently pinned opponents deep in their end, enabling his teammates to play more aggressively on defense.

From LT to Prime Time

Lawrence Taylor ushered in a new era of defense. An outside linebacker for the New York Giants from 1981 to 1993, "LT" was always the best athlete on the field, but his daring style set him apart. Taylor regularly lined up in different spots where he knew he could cause the most mayhem.

Joe Montana was ever aware of defenders like Taylor. While he didn't have the classic build of a quarterback, Montana understood the complexities of the modern game better than anyone. His ability to **anticipate** openings in the defense and deliver pinpoint passes was uncanny. During the 1980s, "Super Joe" won four Super Bowls and formed a dynamic duo with Jerry Rice. When he came out of college in 1985, Rice didn't impress anyone with his speed. But he ran precise pass routes and was an excellent runner once he caught the ball. Rice has broken all of Don Hutson's marks.

Deion Sanders was the answer to receivers like Rice. "Prime Time" was a cornerback with breathtaking speed. His amazing coverage skills took away half the field from opposing quarterbacks.

Do any current players fit the bill as football **trendsetters**? Michael Vick is leading a new breed of quarterbacks who combine passing and

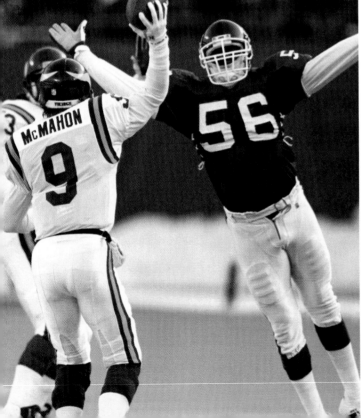

Lawrence Taylor (#56) made outside linebacker one of football's most glamorous positions.

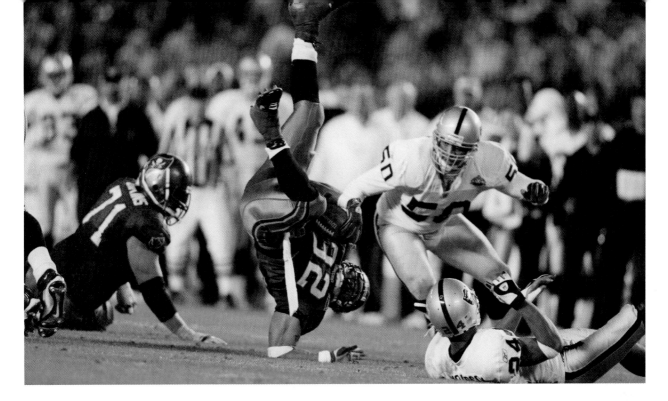

running skills with devastating effectiveness. Marshall Faulk has put a new spin on the running back position with his awesome receiving skills. Jevon Kearse is a defensive end who is athletic enough to play free safety.

This trio is the latest in a legacy of stars that have pushed football's evolution in unexpected directions. Who's next on the list? That's impossible to say. But remember that football's pioneers throughout the years were once kids like you. Many scored their first touchdown or made their first tackle in a cow pasture or city park. At the time, they didn't know they were headed for greatness. They simply loved football. But that's how many of the game's movers and shakers got their start. And it's why football's next great pioneer could be a friend down the street or a classmate on the school bus—or you.

Michael Pittman (#32) of the Buccaneers gets upended in Super Bowl XXXVII. Tampa Bay went on to win 48–21.

51

Timeline

1827	Students at Harvard begin playing an annual rugby match known as "Bloody Monday."
1880	The line of scrimmage is introduced.
1882	The modern system of downs is instituted, and chalk lines are drawn on the field to keep track of yardage.
1889	Walter Camp chooses the first college All-American team.
1902	The Rose Bowl is played for the first time.
1897	Touchdowns are increased in value to six points.
1906	The forward pass is legalized, and mass plays are banned.
1909	Field goals are reduced in value to three points.
1922	The American Professional Football Association changes its name to the National Football League.
1925	The East-West Shrine Bowl is played for the first time.
1934	The NFL reduces the size of the football to the model still used today.
1939	Helmets are made mandatory in college football.
1946	Kenny Washington, then Woody Strode, Marion Motley, and Bill Willis, become the first African-Americans to play in the NFL since 1933.
1954	The NFL passes a rule stating all players must wear facemasks, though veterans are allowed to continue without them.
1960	Pete Rozelle is named NFL Commissioner.

1965	Penalty flags are changed from white to yellow.
1969	Joe Namath leads the New York Jets to an upset victory over the Baltimore Colts in Super Bowl III.
1973	Mouth guards become mandatory in college.
1978	The NFL expands its schedule from fourteen to sixteen games.
1986	The NFL uses instant replay to review calls during games for the first time.
1995	The Carolina Panthers and Jacksonville Jaguars join the NFL.
1997	Charles Woodson of Michigan becomes the first full-time defensive player to win the Heisman Trophy.
1998	The Bowl Championship Series is introduced to college football.
2002	The Houston Texans join the NFL, and the league reorganizes with four divisions in each conference.

Glossary

aerial—moving in the air

anticipate—to imagine something before it happens

audible—a football term for when the quarterback changes the play at the line of scrimmage

civic—connected with the duties and obligations of belonging to a community

coordinated—able to move and use your body skillfully

degenerate—to develop into a worse condition

discourage—to try to stop someone from doing something

elusive—difficult to find or catch

forward pass—a pass thrown forward. Forward passes are legal only if attempted from behind the line of scrimmage.

infraction—a failure to obey a rule

ingenuity—cleverness and originality

lateral—a football term describing a backward pass

mettle—courage, spirit, or strength of character

mythical—being widely known and considered wonderful, like a myth

negotiate—to talk things over until an agreement is reached

overtime—in football, a term for how a game tied after regulation is decided. The NFL plays "sudden death," in which the first team that scores wins.

prominent—distinguished or well known

reinstate—to bring something back into use

sack—a football term describing when a quarterback is tackled behind the line of scrimmage

smorgasbord—a wide variety

symbol—something that stands for something else

tactic—a method or course of action

tenacity—the quality of sticking to a plan or decision without giving up

topsy-turvy—in a confused or chaotic state

trendsetter—someone who makes a new trend popular

valor—courage, especially shown in war

To Find Out More

Books

Anderson, Dave. *The Story of Football*. New York, NY: William Morrow and Company, Inc., 1997.

Owens, Thomas. *Football Stadiums*. Brookfield, CT: The Millbrook Press, 2001.

Stewart, Mark. *Football: A History of the Gridiron Game*. Danbury, CT: Franklin Watts, 1998.

Stewart, Mark. *The Super Bowl*. Danbury, CT: Franklin Watts, 2002.

Any of the football biographies in the New Wave series by Mark Stewart published by the Millbrook Press.

Organizations and Online Sites

College Football Hall of Fame
http://collegefootball.org
Official site of the College Football Hall of Fame. Learn about all of the hall's members through detailed biographies and statistics.

http://nflfans.com/
Visit here to read all the latest news on the NFL, much of it from the fan's perspective.

http://www.sfo.com/~csuppes/NFL/misc/index.htm
An interesting site (affiliated with *www.ballparks.com*) devoted to football stadiums, past and present.

National Football League
http://www.nfl.com
Official site of the National Football League. Read about your favorite players and follow links to your favorite teams.

NCAA Football
http://www.ncaafootball.net
Official site of NCAA Football. Get everything—from news and stats to trivia and photos—about college football players and teams nationwide.

Pop Warner Football

http://www.popwarner.com

Official site of Pop Warner Football. Find out about the history of the organization and how to join a team in your area.

Pro Football Hall of Fame

http:/www.profootballhof.com/

Official site of the Pro Football Hall of Fame. Learn about all of the hall's members through detailed biographies and statistics.

A Note on Sources

In researching this book, I tried to reference as many sources as possible. I consulted another author named Mark Stewart, who has written many books on football, including biographies of famous players. I also read other insightful books, such as *Total Football*, *ABC Sports College Football All-Time All-America Team*, and *The Pro Football Chronicle*. Web sites on the Internet, including the one hosted by the National Football League, were helpful as well.

In addition, I drew on my personal knowledge of football. I played in college, and have coached in high school and youth leagues. These experiences have taught me a great deal about the sport.

—Mike Kennedy

Index

Numbers in *italics* indicate illustrations.

About the Author

From Ichiro to the Indy 500 and the Super Bowl to skateboarding, Mike Kennedy has covered it all in the world of sports. A graduate of Franklin & Marshall College, he has profiled athletes such as Sammy Sosa, Tony Hawk, and Venus and Serena Williams. Mike has contributed his expertise to other books by Grolier/Scholastic, including *The World Series*, *The Super Bowl*, and *The NBA Finals*. He is also a co-creator of JockBio.com (*www.jock-bio.com*), a unique website that profiles popular sports personalities.

His other titles in this series are *Baseball*, *Basketball*, *Ice Hockey*, *Roller Hockey*, *Skateboarding*, and *Soccer*.